ALPHA BOOKS

WORLD WAR II

NICOLA BARBER

EVANS BROTHERS LIMITED

This book is based on **1930s** and **1940s** by Ken Hills, first published by Evans Brothers Limited in 1992, but the original texts have been simplified.

Published by Evans Brothers Limited
2A Portman Mansions
Chiltern Street
London W1M 1LE

First published 1994

Typeset by Fleetlines Typesetters, Southend-on-Sea, Essex
Printed in Spain by GRAFO, S.A. – Bilbao

ISBN 0 237 51327 7

Acknowledgements

Maps – Jillian Luff, Bitmap Graphics
Design – Neil Sayer
Editor – Su Swallow
Language adviser – Suzanne Tiburtius

For permission to reproduce copyright material the author and publishers gratefully acknowledge the following:

Cover photographs – (from top) The Illustrated London News Picture Company, The Vintage Magazine Company, Topham, Topham, The Hulton Picture Company.

Page 5 – (from top) Topham, Topham, Topham, Popperfoto; page 6 – (from top) Popperfoto, The Hulton Picture Company, The Vintage Magazine Co, The Vintage Magazine Co; page 7 – The Hulton Picture Company; page 8 – (left) The Hulton Picture Company, (right) Topham; page 9 – (left) Barnaby's Picture Library, (middle, top right) The Hulton Picture Company/The Bettmann Archive, (bottom right) The Illustrated London News Picture Library; page 10 – Topham; page 11 – (left) Penguin Books, (top) The Hulton Picture Company/The Bettmann Archive, (bottom) Topham; page 12 – Topham; page 13 – The Illustrated London News Picture Library; page 14 – (left, right) Topham, (top) The Vintage Magazine Co; page 16 – (top) Topham, (middle) The Hulton Picture Company/The Bettmann Archive, (bottom) Associated Press/Topham; page 17 – (left) Topham, (top right) Barnaby's Picture Library, (bottom right) The Illustrated London News Picture Library; page 18 – Topham; page 19 – The Hulton Picture Company; page 20 – (top left) Colorsport, (bottom left) The Hulton Picture Company, (top right) The Vintage Magazine Co, (bottom right) Topham; page 21 – (left) The Hulton Picture Company, (right) Topham; page 22 – The Hulton Picture Company; page 24 – The Vintage Magazine Co; page 26 – (top) The Hulton Picture Company, (bottom) Ronald Sheridan/Ancient Art and Architecture Collection; page 27 – The Fine Art Society, London/Bridgeman Art Library; page 28 – The Vintage Magazine Co; page 29 – The Vintage Magazine Co; page 30 – (top) The Vintage Magazine Co, (bottom) Topham; page 31 – (top) The Hulton Picture Company, (bottom) Topham; page 32 – The Vintage Magazine Co; page 33 – Topham; page 34 – Topham; page 35 – (top) Topham, (bottom) The Hulton Picture Company; page 36 – (top) The Vintage Magazine Co, (bottom) Imperial War Muesum, London/Bridgeman Art Library; page 37 – (left) Topham, (right) The Hulton Picture Company; page 38 – The Vintage Magazine Co; page 39 – (top) Topham, (bottom) the Hulton Picture Company; page 40 – The Hulton Picture Company; page 41 – (top) The Vintage Magazine Co, (bottom) Topham; page 42 – Topham; page 43 – The Vintage Magazine Co; page 44 – (left) The Vintage Magazine Co, (right) Topham; page 45 – (top) The Hulton Picture Company, (middle) Topham, (bottom) The Hulton Picture Company.

Introduction

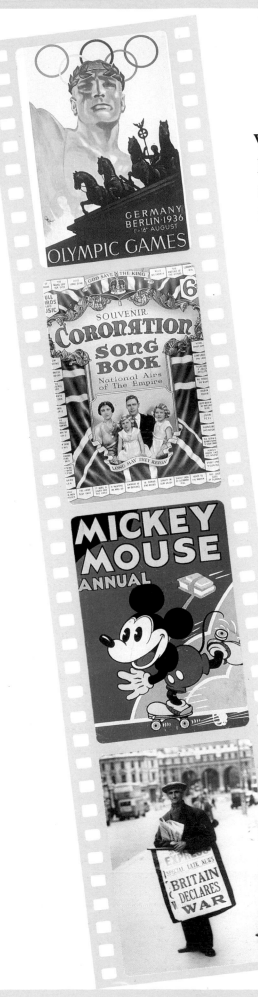

World War II began in September 1939 and ended in 1945. The war started in Europe when the German leader, Adolf Hitler, invaded Poland. Within a week Britain, Australia, New Zealand, South Africa, Canada and France had all declared war on Germany. Many other countries joined the fighting during the six years of the war. Over 55 million people died in the war. Many died in concentration camps. Bombs dropped in air raids also killed many other people.

The war ended when the USA dropped two atomic bombs on Japanese cities. After the war, the leaders of countries all around the world were determined to work for peace. They set up a new organisation called the United Nations to try to prevent more wars in the future.

The pictures on page 5 show:
 Poster advertising 1936 Olympic Games in Berlin
 Cover of British *Coronation Song Book*, 1937
 Cover of *Mickey Mouse Annual*
 Newspaper seller on the day Britain declared war,
   September 3, 1939

The pictures on page 6 show:
 Winston Churchill, the British Prime Minister
 The pilot of an RAF bomber plane
 Nazi tanks stuck in the mud in Russia
 Japanese officials surrendering on the American
   warship *Missouri* at the end of the war

Contents

1933

Jan 30   **Hitler becomes Chancellor of Germany**
Feb 28   **Fire destroys German parliament**
March 20   **Concentration camps in Germany**

New leader for Germany

January 30, Berlin, Germany The new leader of Germany is Adolf Hitler. Hitler is also leader of the Nazi party. The Nazis are enemies of the Communists and Jewish people. Many people are afraid that Hitler will now try to destroy these people.

△ Hitler (centre) with his ministers

Fire burns down German parliament

February 28, Berlin, Germany Fire burnt down the German parliament building last night. The parliament building is called the Reichstag. Chancellor Hitler has blamed the Communists for the fire.

Concentration camps

March 20, Berlin, Germany Places called concentration camps are planned in Germany. Anyone who speaks out against the Nazi government will be put in one of these camps. The first camp has already opened at Dachau.

Countries walk out of League

October 14, Geneva, Switzerland Germany and Japan have walked out of the League of Nations. The League of Nations is an international organisation. It was set up after World War I to try to settle arguments in a peaceful way. But many people now think that the League does not have the power to keep the world at peace.

1934

Austrian Chancellor is killed

July 25, Vienna, Austria The Austrian leader, Chancellor Dollfuss, was killed today. At noon, armed men went into the offices of Dr Dollfuss and shot him. They would not let a doctor in to see him and he bled to death. The armed men were members of the Austrian Nazi party.

The German leader, Adolf Hitler, has said that the German Nazi party had nothing to do with the killing. But many people think that Hitler had something to do with this crime.

▽ The body of the Austrian Chancellor, Dr Dollfuss, is guarded by two soldiers.

Leading Nazis killed

June 30, Munich, Germany A leading Nazi, Ernst Roehm, has been killed. Some people think that other members of the Nazi party have also died elsewhere in Germany. It seems that Hitler himself ordered the murder of these people.

△ Adolf Hitler with some of his Nazi supporters

News in brief . . .

German children become Nazis

Germany When German boys are ten years old, they have to join the Young Peoples' Movement. They wear Nazi uniforms and learn to parade like soldiers. When they join the Movement they have to stand under a Nazi flag and say: "Under this flag, I swear to give all my strength to Adolf

△ German boys in the Young Peoples' Movement

Hitler, the man who saved our country. I am willing and ready to die for him, so help me God."

A German greeting

Germany The Nazi government has ordered all Germans to greet each other in a new way. When two people meet they must hold up their right arms and say "Heil Hitler!" which means "Hail, Hitler!".

Shorts at Wimbledon

May, London, England Women tennis players will be allowed to wear shorts instead of skirts at Wimbledon this year. Many male officials are

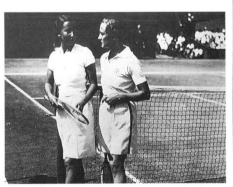

△ Women tennis players wearing shorts

upset by this new rule. They say that shorts are unsuitable for women to wear. They think that women who play at Wimbledon should set a good example.

Dillinger dead

July 22, Chicago, USA The bank robber and murderer, John Dillinger, is dead. John Dillinger has killed 16 people. The police shot him as he came out of a cinema.

▽ John Dillinger, the bank robber and murderer

Queen Mary launched

September 26, Glasgow, Scotland The ship called the *Queen Mary* was launched today. The *Queen Mary* is the first ship ever to weigh more than 75,000 tonnes.

▽ The launch of the *Queen Mary*

1935

March 16   Hitler tears up Versailles treaty
May   Threat of war in East Africa
October 3   Italy invades Abyssinia

Hitler tears up treaty

March 16, Berlin, Germany Hitler has torn up the Versailles Treaty. This was the agreement that ended World War I. The treaty said that Germany could have a small army and navy, and no airforce. Now Hitler has ignored the treaty and started to build up Germany's armed forces.

War in East Africa

May, East Africa It seems likely that there will be a war in East Africa. The Italian leader, Mussolini, has sent troops to Italian East Africa. They are now on the border between East Africa and Abyssinia.

△ The Abyssinian army gets ready for war.

Italy invades Abyssinia

October 3, East Africa Italian troops crossed the border into Abyssinia this morning. The Italians have modern weapons. Many of the Abyssinians only have spears and bows and arrows to fight with.

△ Italian troops leave for East Africa.

News in brief . . .

Dust storms in America

April 15, USA Strong winds have blown clouds of dust across farmland in America (see right). The dust has ruined many crops. Thousands of people have left their homes because they cannot grow any food.

A new world record

September 3, Bonneville Salt Flats, Utah, USA Sir Malcolm Campbell has set a new world record for the fastest speed on land. He went at 301 miles per hour in his car *Bluebird*. This is the eighth time Campbell has broken the world record.

First performance of *Porgy and Bess*

September 30, Boston, USA The opera *Porgy and Bess* has its first performance today. *Porgy and Bess* is by George Gershwin. There are many fine tunes in the opera, including the song *Summertime*.

Good books for everyone

July, London Penguin books are in the shops. 'Penguin' is the name of a new family of books published by Mr Allen Lane. The books are paperbacks. They cost only sixpence (two new pence) each.

Nazis ban jazz music

October, Berlin The Nazis have banned all jazz music played by black people or Jewish people in Germany. The Nazis say that this jazz music has a bad effect on young Germans.

THE THEATRE GUILD PRESENTS

PORGY and BESS

MUSIC BY GEORGE GERSHWIN

LIBRETTO BY DUBOSE HEYWARD

LYRICS BY DUBOSE HEYWARD and IRA GERSHWIN

PRODUCTION DIRECTED BY ROUBEN MAMOULIAN

GERSHWIN PUBLISHING CORPORATION & NEW DAWN MUSIC CORPORATION
609 Fifth Avenue, New York, N.Y. 10017
CHAPPELL & CO. INC.

1936

January 20	Britain has new king
May 9	Italy occupies Abyssinia
July 31	Civil War in Spain
December 10	King Edward VIII abdicates
December 12	George VI is new British king

New king for Britain

January 20, London, England King George V has died. He had been on the throne for 25 years. The king's eldest son, Edward, becomes King Edward VIII.

▽ A poster showing the power of American industry

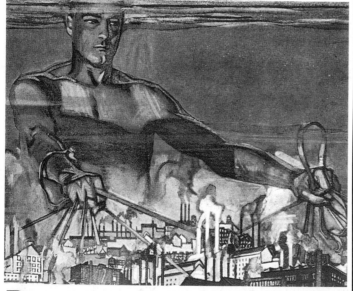

Roosevelt wins again

November 3, Washington, USA The American people have elected Franklin D. Roosevelt to be their president for the second time. Roosevelt has been president since 1933. He is very popular with the American people.

A king in love

December 10, London, England The new king is in love with Mrs Wallis Simpson. She is an American who has been married twice before. The king is not allowed to marry someone who has been married before. So King Edward VIII has decided to abdicate. This means that he has given up the throne. His brother will become the new king instead.

Many people have tried to persuade King Edward to give up Mrs Simpson. But he will not change his mind. He has chosen to give up the throne in order to marry Mrs Simpson.

The new royal family

December 12, London, England King Edward VIII has left the country. His new title is the Duke of Windsor. His brother is now the new King George VI. King George and his wife Queen Elizabeth have two daughters, Princess Elizabeth and Princess Margaret. Princess Elizabeth is ten years old.

Civil war in Spain

SPANISH CIVIL WAR (July/August 1936)

N

Santander
Guernica
FRANCE
Bilbao
Vigo
Burgos
(Nationalist Government Headquarters)
CATALONIA
Salamanca
Barcelona
Madrid
PORTUGAL
SPAIN
Minorca
Majorca
Lisbon
Ibiza
Seville
Granada
ATLANTIC
Cadiz
OCEAN
Gibraltar
(British)
Tangier
0 km 250
SPANISH MOROCCO

Initial advance of Nationalists
Nationalist territory
Republican territory

July 31, Spain A civil war has started in Spain. A civil war is when people from the same country fight against each other. The Spanish army has attacked the Spanish government and its supporters. The leader of the Spanish army is General Franco. He says that the government is turning Spain into a Communist country. He has started a new political party to fight against Communism. It is called the Nationalist party.

People who are on the side of the Spanish government are called Republicans. The Republicans have formed an army of their own. But the Republican army does not have as many weapons as Franco's army. Fighting between the Republicans and the Nationalists is going on all over Spain.

Italy occupies Abyssinia

May 9, Abyssinia Italian soldiers have reached Addis Ababa, the capital of Abyssinia. The Italians are in control of Addis Ababa. This means that the country of Abyssinia now belongs to Italy. The emperor of Abyssinia has escaped and gone abroad. The king of Italy will now be called 'Emperor of Abyssinia'.

German troops enter Rhineland

March 6, Rhineland German soldiers have gone into the Rhineland. The Rhineland is an area of land between France and Germany. After World War I this area was used to keep the two countries apart. There were to be no troops in this area. People are very unhappy that the German troops have ignored this agreement. Now many people think that Germany wants to start another war.

△ Republican fighters in Barcelona

News in brief . . .

A new car for Germany

February 26, Wolfsburg, Germany Hitler has opened a new factory in Wolfsburg. The factory will make a cheap family car. This car will be called 'The People's Car'. Its German name is *Volkswagen*.

▷ The new German car, the *Volkswagen*

Jesse Owens wins medals

August 15, Berlin, Germany The eleventh Olympic Games ended today. The black American runner, Jesse Owens, won four gold medals. The Nazis are very angry about this. The Nazis say that white people are better than black people. But a black runner has shown everyone that he is the best in the world.

▽ Jesse Owens

OLYMPIAN

JESSE OWENS 1936

USA 25

King Edward's speech

December 11, London, England Edward VIII made his last speech as king this evening. The speech was broadcast on the radio. This is part of what he said: "I want you to understand that in making up my mind I did not forget the country or the Empire which as Prince of Wales and lately as king, I have for 25 years tried to serve. But you must believe me when I tell you that I have found it impossible to carry the heavy bur-

△ King Edward makes his last speech.

den of responsibility and to discharge my duties as king as I would wish to do without the help and support of the woman I love . . ."

1937

Fighting in Spain

February, Spain People from other countries are fighting in the Civil War in Spain. Italian and German troops are helping General Franco and the Nationalists. The Russians are helping the Republicans.

Guernica bombed

April 26, northern Spain This is how a reporter described what he found in the city of Guernica after the German bombing:

'In the Plaza, surrounded almost by a wall of fire, were about a hundred refugees. They were wailing and weeping and rocking to and fro. One middle-aged man spoke English. He told me, 'At four, before the market closed, many aeroplanes came. They dropped bombs. Some came low and shot bullets into the streets. . .'

(Noel Monks, *Eyewitness*, Frederick Muller 1955)

Spanish city destroyed

April 30, northern Spain Bombs have destroyed the city of Guernica (see map page 13). Guernica is in part of northern Spain held by the Republicans. The bombs were dropped by German planes. The Germans are fighting on the side of General Franco and the Nationalists.

It was market day in Guernica when the Germans dropped the bombs. Fires and explosions killed over 2000 people in Guernica. The people had no warning that the Germans were going to attack. People all round the world are shocked and angry about the bombing.

George VI crowned

May 12, London, England King George and Queen Elizabeth were crowned this morning in Westminster Abbey. The king and queen's two daughters watched the crowning. Afterwards the royal family went back to Buckingham Palace and waved from the balcony to the huge crowds below.

News in brief . . .

Giant airship explodes

May 6, Lakehurst Airfield, USA The giant airship *Hindenburg* has exploded. The German airship had just crossed the Atlantic Ocean. It was about to stop at its mooring mast. Suddenly the airship caught fire and the gas inside the airship exploded. All 34 people on board died in the flames.

Only last year the *Hindenburg* had set a new record for the fastest crossing of the Atlantic. It had crossed the ocean in under two days. The Germans were hoping to start a regular passenger service across the Atlantic Ocean.

The terror of war

October, Paris, France The Spanish artist, Pablo Picasso, has painted a picture in protest at the bombing of Guernica earlier this year. His picture reminds people of the terror of war.

▷ Picasso's painting, *Guernica*

New boxing champion

June 3, New York, USA The American boxer, Joe Louis (see right), is the new heavyweight boxing champion of the world. Joe Louis is the first black boxer to be champion for 22 years.

1938

March 14   German troops invade Austria
September 27   Hitler threatens war
September 30   Munich meeting
November 11   Germans attack Jews

Hitler threatens war

September 27, Germany Adolf Hitler wants parts of Czechoslovakia to become part of Germany. The British Prime Minister, Neville Chamberlain, has gone to Munich to try to persuade Hitler not to go to war.

△ A picture of Adolf Hitler on a German poster

△ Prime Minister Neville Chamberlain (right) with Adolf Hitler

Churchill says, "Don't give in"

September 28, London, England A member of the British parliament, Winston Churchill, has said that Chamberlain should not give in to Hitler. He says that Britain and France should fight if Germany attacks Czechoslovakia. Many people agree with Winston Churchill.

△ Preparing for war in London. Sandbags protect a police station against bombs.

Chamberlain returns from Munich

△ Neville Chamberlain returns from Munich.

September 30, London, England Crowds of people welcomed Prime Minister Chamberlain as he came back from Munich this evening. Chamberlain waved a piece of paper signed by Hitler and himself. He said that Britain and Germany would not go to war. "It is peace for our time," he said.

The leaders of France, Italy and Britain have agreed that Germany can take over parts of Czechoslovakia. In return, Hitler has said that he will leave the Czech people in peace. Many people are relieved because a war now looks unlikely. But the Czech people are unhappy about this agreement.

German troops invade Austria

March 14, Vienna, Austria German troops have crossed into Austria. People cheered as Hitler drove through the streets of Vienna, the Austrian capital.

The Austrian leader, Seyss Inquart, is a member of the Nazi party. He invited the Germans to invade Austria. Many Austrians would like their country to become part of Germany.

Germany is now the most powerful country in Europe.

Germans attack Austrian Jews

March 18, Vienna, Austria The Germans have attacked the Jews living in Austria. The Germans have said that no Jewish person is allowed to be a lawyer, doctor or teacher.

△ The Nazis have smashed the windows of shops owned by Jews.

Danger of war over Czechoslovakia

May 20, Prague, Czechoslovakia Once again, there is a threat of war. German troops now surround Czechoslovakia on three sides (see map). There are many Germans living in Czechoslovakia. They say that the Czech people treat them badly. They have asked Germany for protection.

If Germany does invade Czechoslovakia it will break the agreement made between Chamberlain and Hitler. It is hard to see how Britain and France could avoid going to war against Germany if this happens.

Franco winning Spanish war

April 15, Spain General Franco claims that he is winning the Spanish Civil War. It seems that the Republicans must face defeat.

'Kristallnacht'

November 11, Berlin, Germany Two nights ago mobs attacked Jews all over Germany. Thousands of Jewish shops were smashed and robbed. There was so much broken glass on the streets that the Germans have called it "Kristallnacht" — 'the night of broken glass'.

GERMANY ATTACKS CZECHOSLOVAKIA

N

DENMARK
USSR
BRITAIN
London NETH.
BELGIUM
Danzig
Berlin
GERMANY
POLAND
Rhine
Paris
Prague
CZECHOSLOVAKIA
SWITZERLAND
Vienna
AUSTRIA
HUNGARY
FRANCE
Danube
YUGOSLAVIA
ITALY

0   km   500

German-speaking areas of Czechoslovakia

News in brief . . .

Snow White success

January, Hollywood, USA
Walt Disney's new film *Snow White and the Seven Dwarfs* is a great success. *Snow White* is the first full-length cartoon film to be made.

Italy wins World Cup

June 19, Paris, France The Italian football team has won the World Cup in the final in Paris.

Britain orders more planes

July 15, London, England The British government has ordered 1000 new planes for the Royal Air Force. The planes are called Spitfires.

▽ A Spitfire plane

British get gas masks

September 20, London, England Everyone in Britain is to get a free gas mask. The masks are to protect against poison gas from bombs.

▽ Children carry their new gas masks.

1939

March 15	Germany invades Czechoslovakia
March 31	Hitler threatens Poland
August 23	Russia and Germany sign agreement
September 1	Germany invades Poland
September 3	Britain and France declare war on Germany

Hitler invades Czechoslovakia

March 15, Berlin, Germany Hitler has invaded Czechoslovakia. Two days ago he sent a list of demands to the Czech government. The Czechs did not give in to Hitler's demands. So Hitler has used this as an excuse to move troops into Czechoslovakia.

△ Germans cheer as Hitler returns to Berlin after the invasion of Czechoslovakia.

Czech people weep as Germans enter Prague

March 16, Prague, Czechoslovakia Czechs showed their anger as the Germans entered their capital city, Prague, today. Some people stood silently, some hissed and booed, some shook their fists. Some wept to see the hated enemy in their country. The German soldiers forced the people to give the Nazi salute. All cafés, restaurants, theatres and cinemas are to be closed.

△ People in Prague are forced to salute like Nazis.

Czech invasion shocks the world

March 17 Hitler's invasion of Czechoslovakia has shocked the whole world. Only six months ago, Hitler promised in Munich to leave Czechoslovakia alone. Now he has made the country part of Germany. Both the British and French governments have sent letters to Berlin protesting about the hostile German invasion.

Russia and Germany sign agreement

August 23, Moscow, USSR Russia and Germany have signed an agreement not to go to war against each other. This is bad news for Britain and France. If necessary, they were hoping to persuade Russia to join them against Germany.

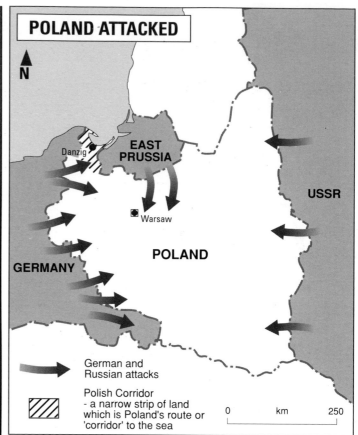

POLAND ATTACKED

Danzig
EAST PRUSSIA
Warsaw
GERMANY
POLAND
USSR

German and Russian attacks

Polish Corridor
- a narrow strip of land which is Poland's route or 'corridor' to the sea

0   km   250

Hitler threatens Poland

March 31, Berlin, Germany Hitler is now threatening Poland. He wants the Poles to give up the city of Danzig to Germany. Danzig used to be a German city. But it became part of Poland after World War I. Now Hitler wants the city back.

Britain and France have promised to help Poland if Germany attacks.

The People's Dispensary for Sick Animals of the Poor. Inc.
GAS PROOF SHELTER
~FOR~
DOGS. CATS & OTHER SMALL ANIMALS

△ A shelter for animals to protect them from gas in an air raid

Europe gets ready for war

August 31, London, England Europe is getting ready for war. In Poland, France and Britain thousands of young men have left their jobs to join the armed forces.

Germany invades Poland

September 1, Poland German troops invaded Poland early this morning. They pulled down barriers along the border and crossed into Poland.

Russia attacks Poland

September 17, Poland Russian troops have invaded Poland. They are trying to occupy as much of the country as they can before the Germans get there. The Polish army is trapped between the two invaders.

Britain and France go to war

September 3, London, England Britain and France are at war with Germany. Prime Minister Chamberlain gave the news to the British people in a radio broadcast at 11.15 this morning.

British troops land in France

September 27, France About 150,000 troops have landed in France. They will help the French to fight against the Germans.

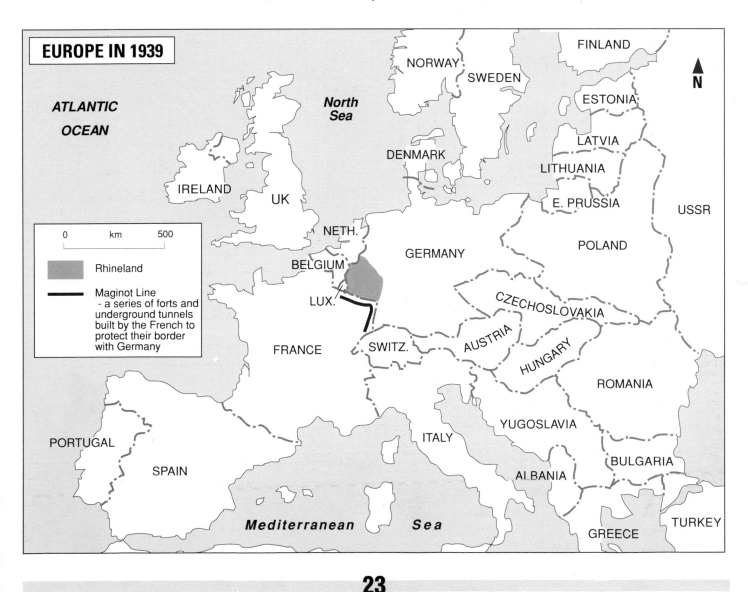

EUROPE IN 1939

ATLANTIC OCEAN

North Sea

NORWAY
SWEDEN
FINLAND
ESTONIA
LATVIA
LITHUANIA
E. PRUSSIA
USSR
DENMARK
IRELAND
UK
NETH.
BELGIUM
LUX.
GERMANY
POLAND
CZECHOSLOVAKIA
AUSTRIA
SWITZ.
HUNGARY
FRANCE
ROMANIA
YUGOSLAVIA
ITALY
BULGARIA
PORTUGAL
SPAIN
ALBANIA
GREECE
TURKEY
Mediterranean Sea

0 km 500

Rhineland

Maginot Line
- a series of forts and underground tunnels built by the French to protect their border with Germany

N

Spanish Civil War ends

March 28, Madrid, Spain General Franco has won the Civil War in Spain. He has beaten the Republicans and the war is over. But there are many problems for Franco. The war destroyed many towns and cities as well as factories. Many farm animals died. The whole country needs rebuilding, but Spain is now a poor country.

British children moved to safety

September 2, London, England Many British children from the towns and cities are moving to the safety of the countryside. The children are leaving their homes to stay with families in the countryside. This is because the Germans are likely to bomb the cities. The countryside is safer.

German battleship sinks

December 17, Montevideo, Uruguay The German battleship, the *Graf Spee*, has sunk. Her own crew blew the ship up. This is because British warships were waiting for the *Graf Spee* as she left the harbour in Montevideo. There was no escape for the German ship. The Royal Navy has been looking for the *Graf Spee* for weeks.

Children moved from London

September 1, London, England Moving people away from a dangerous place to a safer place is called evacuation. This is a description of the evacuation of some children from a school in London: 'I watched the schoolteachers calling out their names and tying luggage labels on their coats, checking their parcels to see there were warm and clean clothes . . . mothers and fathers were saying goodbye, straightening the girls' hair, getting the boys to blow their noses and lightly and quickly kissing them . . . There was quite a long wait before this small army got its orders . . . to move off . . .

Labelled and lined up the children began to move out of the school.'

(Hilde Marchant, *Women and Children Last*, published by Victor Gollancz Ltd, 1941)

1940

May 10	Churchill new British leader
May 13	Germans advance into France
June 4	Rescue from Dunkirk
June 19	Germans enter Paris
August 20	Battle of Britain

German invasions

May 10, Oslo, Norway German troops invaded Norway and Denmark in April. The Germans took the Danes by surprise. The Danes were not ready to fight so they surrendered to the Germans. There was fighting in Oslo, the Norwegian capital. But a Norwegian Nazi called Quisling took control of the country for the Germans. Now most of Norway is controlled by the Germans. British and French troops have landed in Norway to try to drive the Germans out. But so far they have not succeeded.

New leader for Britain

May 10, London, England Winston Churchill has replaced Neville Chamberlain as leader of Britain. Many people blame Neville Chamberlain for Britain's failure to save Norway from the Germans. Winston Churchill will form a National Government made up of people from all political parties.

German advances continue

May 13, France German troops are still advancing across Europe. They have invaded Holland, Luxembourg and Belgium. Germany is now attacking France. Britain and France are now making plans to fight back.

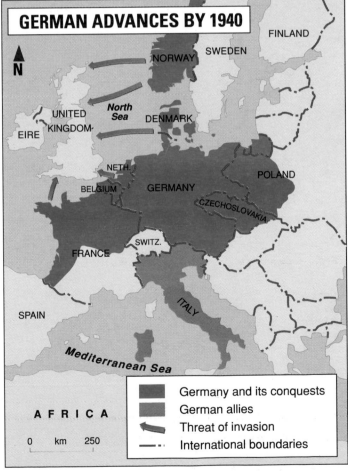

By 1940 the Germans had taken much of Europe.

British army trapped in Dunkirk

May 29, France German forces have reached the French coast along the Channel. The British army is trapped in the port of Dunkirk. The only way out is by sea.

Cave discovery

November 1, Lascaux, France Some French boys have made an amazing discovery. They were catching rabbits when they saw a gap in some rocks. They went through the gap and found a cave. Paintings covered the cave walls. Experts say that the paintings are 15,000 years old.

Rescue from Dunkirk

June 4, London, England Hundreds of little ships have gone to the rescue of the British army. The ships sailed across the Channel to Dunkirk. They brought back over 300,000 British troops to Britain.

△ British troops waiting at Dunkirk
▽ Cave paintings in Lascaux

Paris falls to Germans

June 19, London, England The Germans have occupied Paris. The Germans now control much of France. But some French people are determined to go on fighting against the Germans. This movement against the Germans is called the Resistance. The Resistance is led by General Charles de Gaulle from London.

RAF is unbeaten

August 20, London, England The Royal Air Force (RAF) is fighting a fierce war against the German airforce (the Luftwaffe). German troops are waiting to invade Britain. But they must wait until the Luftwaffe has destroyed the British defences.

RAF saves Britain

September 19, London, England The RAF says it shot down 185 Luftwaffe planes in air battles on September 15. The RAF seems to have beaten the Luftwaffe in the 'Battle of Britain'. Hitler has given up his plans to invade Britain. The RAF has saved Britain.

△ A painting called *The Battle of Britain* by Paul Nash

News in brief . . .

Roosevelt wins again

November 5, Washington, USA Once again, Americans have voted for Franklin D. Roosevelt to be their president. This is the third time that Roosevelt has been elected. This is good news for Britain because Roosevelt is a strong supporter of its war efforts.

Children go home

January 30, London, England When the war started last September many children from the cities went to live in the countryside. People thought it would be safer there. But many children did not like living in the countryside. They missed their parents. So many have now gone home, back to the cities.

Tragedy in the Atlantic

September 22, London, England There has been a tragedy in the Atlantic Ocean. The ship *City of Benares* was sailing to America to take many children away from the dangers of war in Britain. But a German submarine sunk the *City of Benares*. Ships have picked up 46 children, but 306 have drowned.

Pets at war

"Send your pets to the country if you can. If you cannot, remember that your dog will not be allowed to go into a public air raid shelter with you. So don't take him shopping with you. Take him for walks near home, so that you can get back quickly.

Cats can take care of themselves far better than you can. Your cat will probably meet you when you get into the shelter."

(BBC broadcast on how to look after your pets during wartime.)

Nights underground

September 30, London, England Thousands of people in London spend their nights in Underground stations. They

△ People sleeping in the Underground

are sheltering from the German air raids. But the Underground stations are very dirty, as this girl describes:

"Dirt abounds everywhere. The floors are never swept and are filthy. People are sleeping on piles of rubbish."

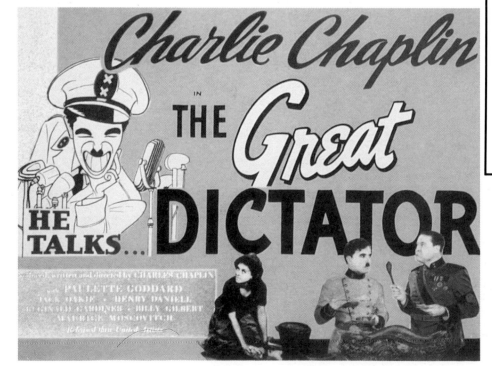

The Great Dictator

November 11, London, England *The Great Dictator* is a new film by Charlie Chaplin. The film makes fun of the German leader, Adolf Hitler.

1941

May 27   Royal Navy sinks the *Bismarck*
December 2   German troops freeze in Russian winter
December 7   Japanese bomb Pearl Harbor

Germans invade Russia

October 26, Moscow, USSR   In June, Hitler attacked the USSR. Three million troops with 3000 tanks crossed the Russian border. The Russian leader, Stalin, ordered people to burn or destroy anything that would be useful to the Germans including crops, animals and machines. The Germans are now moving towards the capital of the USSR, Moscow. But rain has made all the roads very muddy. The Germans are struggling to keep moving forwards.

Germans freeze in Russian winter

December 2, Moscow, USSR   The German army is freezing in the cold Russian winter. Russian troops are now attacking the Germans and forcing them to go back.

The war at sea

May 27, North Atlantic Ocean   The Royal Navy sank the huge German battleship the *Bismarck* today. The *Bismarck* had attacked many of the ships that carried food and other supplies from America to Britain.

△ A painting called *The End of the Bismarck* by Charles E. Turner

Attack at Pearl Harbor

December 7, Honolulu, Hawaii In a surprise attack, Japanese planes have bombed American ships at Pearl Harbor in Hawaii. The bombs killed over 2000 people. The USA and Britain have declared war on Japan.

△ Japanese planes attack American ships at Pearl Harbor.

War in the desert

April 11, Libya Earlier this year troops from Britain and other friendly countries (called the Allies) advanced against the Italian army in North Africa. Now German soldiers have taken over from the Italian army. The Germans are attacking the Allied troops fiercely.

Germans retreat in Africa

December 10, Libya The Allies are fighting back against the German army. They have pushed the Germans back to where they were in April.

The Japanese advance

December 25, Hong Kong Japanese forces have landed in Thailand, Malaya and the Philippines. They now control the American island of Guam in the Pacific Ocean. Today the Japanese have also taken Hong Kong.

Women at work

December 30, Britain Women are doing the jobs left by male workers who have gone to fight in the war. The government first asked women to help in March. Now, some women are working in factories, others are working on farms. Many women have also joined the armed forces. They have to work very hard, but are glad to help. Many women have never done this kind of work before.

△ Women workers on the farms are called land girls.

News in brief . . .

Amy Johnson missing

January 8, London, England Amy Johnson is missing. People think she may have drowned in the Thames when her plane crashed. Amy Johnson became famous when she flew on her own from Britain to Australia before the war.

First boy scout dies

January 8, London, England Lord Baden Powell has died. He was 83 years old. Lord Baden Powell started the Boy Scouts in 1908 and the Girl Guides in 1910.

Comfort in the Underground

February 28, London, England Conditions have improved for people in the Underground. Every night people shelter in Underground stations from the bombs. Now the government has put in bunk beds for people to sleep on. Some stations have cookers and kettles for people to make food and drinks.

Britain and America sign agreement

August 14, London, England President Roosevelt and Prime Minister Churchill have held a secret meeting at sea. They signed an agreement to continue fighting until they beat their enemies. The agreement is called the Atlantic Charter.

△ Roosevelt and Churchill meet on board HMS *Prince of Wales*.

The Blitz in London

May 31, London, England The German bombing of London is called the Blitz. In the Blitz, bombs have damaged nearly four million houses in Britain and destroyed about 200,000 more. Many thousands of people have no home.

▽ Many houses have been damaged in the Blitz.

1942

RAF bombs Cologne

May 31, Cologne, Germany More than a thousand RAF planes have dropped bombs on the city of Cologne. The bombs destroyed most of the city.

Germans in Stalingrad

November 23, Stalingrad, USSR German troops have been in Stalingrad since August and are dying of hunger and cold. Most of the city is in ruins.

△ Ruined houses in Stalingrad

△ Ruins in the centre of the city

△ The Russians left their guns behind.

△ German troops advance

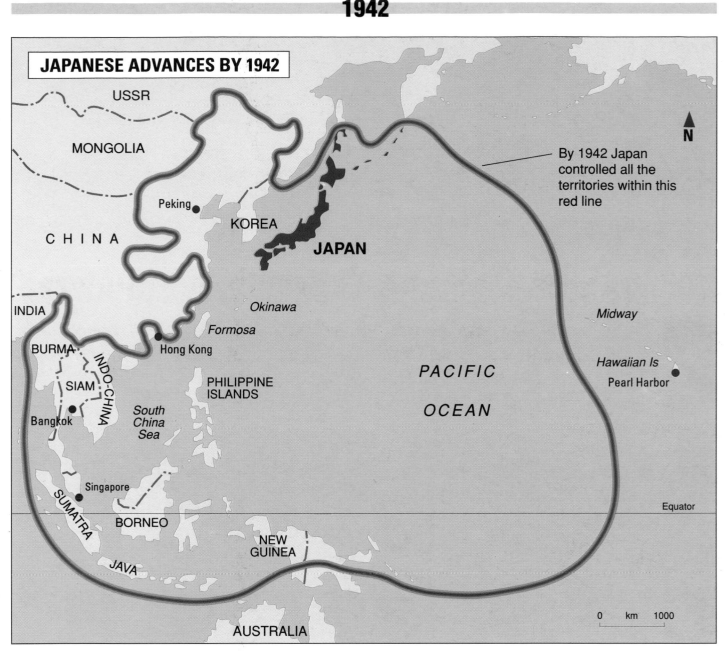

JAPANESE ADVANCES BY 1942

USSR

MONGOLIA

Peking

KOREA

C H I N A

JAPAN

By 1942 Japan controlled all the territories within this red line

N

Okinawa

Formosa

INDIA

Midway

BURMA

Hong Kong

Hawaiian Is
Pearl Harbor

SIAM

INDO-CHINA

PHILIPPINE
ISLANDS

PACIFIC

Bangkok

South
China
Sea

OCEAN

SUMATRA

Singapore

Equator

BORNEO

JAVA

NEW
GUINEA

0   km   1000

AUSTRALIA

Japan marches on

May 10, Philippine Islands The Japanese army has had many successes in the Pacific and southeast Asia. The Japanese control Singapore and the Philippines. Now they are threatening India.

British win in Africa

November 2, Cairo, Egypt The British have won a ten-day battle against the Germans at El Alamein in Africa. Under their new commander, General Montgomery, British troops are now chasing the German troops as they retreat westwards.

▽ General Montgomery (centre)

1943

German army retreats

December 31, USSR The German army is retreating from Russia. The Germans have not been able to defeat the Russian army. The Russian army stopped the Germans from capturing Kursk in July. Then the Russians took the city of Kiev from the Germans. Now the Germans are retreating. The Russians are driving the enemy out of their country. So far they have pushed the Germans back 300 kilometres.

Victory in North Africa

May 13, Tunisia The Allied troops have won a victory in North Africa. The German forces were trapped by the Allies and have given up.

Invasion of Italy

September 3, Messina, Italy The British army and its Allies have landed in southern Italy. They are fighting the German army in Italy. The government of Italy wants to make peace with the Allies.

△ The British army cross the Sangro River in Italy.

The war against Japan

December 29, Solomon Islands, Pacific Ocean The Americans are slowly capturing the islands around Japan. But the Japanese soldiers fight until they are killed. They do not give up. Many Americans have also died.

Allies fight on in Italy

December 31, Italy The American and British armies are still fighting the Germans in Italy. The Germans are fighting very fiercely. The Allies have reached a line of German defences across Italy. This is called the Gustav Line. Progress has been very slow, and the Gustav Line has stopped the Allies advancing any further.

Allied leaders meet in Persia

November 28, Tehran, Persia The three leaders of the Allied forces are meeting in Persia. They are planning what to do next in the war.

△ Stalin, Roosevelt and Churchill in Persia

Germans attack ghetto

June 30, Warsaw, Poland On April 19, German troops attacked the Jewish ghetto in Warsaw. The ghetto is the part of the city where the Germans made all the Jewish people live. Now the Germans are taking the Jews to concentration camps. About 7000 Jews have died fighting the Germans.

▷ German troops force Polish Jews out of the ghetto in Warsaw.

1944

US General to lead Allies

January 16, London, England The American General, Dwight D. Eisenhower, is to lead the Allies. Eisenhower is known as 'Ike'. The Allies are getting ready to invade Europe and attack the Germans.

▷ Eisenhower with some of his troops

'D-Day' in France

June 6, Normandy, France Today is 'D-Day' and the Allies have landed in France. The Germans are fighting fiercely. But the Allies have been fighting back.

Allies advance in France

August 20, Falaise, France On August 2, American troops advanced into France. Now, 50,000 Germans are trapped by the Americans around the town of Falaise.

△ A painting by Barnett Freedman showing the Allies landing in France.

Plans for peace

September 16, Quebec, Canada The Allies are planning a better world when the war is over. President Roosevelt and Prime Minister Churchill have agreed to start a new organisation for keeping the world at peace. It will be called the United Nations Organisation.

Paris is free

August 26, Paris, France Paris is free. The Allied troops have forced the Germans to leave. French soldiers were the first to enter the city. People cheered and waved as General Charles de Gaulle led the troops.

△ General Charles de Gaulle in Paris

The war in Italy

December 9, Rimini, Italy The Allied forces have now pushed the Germans into northern Italy. But many Allied troops are now leaving Italy and going to fight on the borders of Germany.

Thousands killed in Warsaw

October 9, Warsaw, Poland It is thought that the Germans have killed 200,000 Polish people in Warsaw. The Poles tried to attack the Germans. But the Germans killed the Poles and destroyed all the buildings in Warsaw.

△ The ruins of Warsaw

Russian victories

December 1, Belgrade, Yugoslavia The Russian army has had many victories this year. The Russians have beaten the Germans in Romania, Bulgaria, Hungary and Yugoslavia. As the Germans have left, the Russians have put in their own rulers in these countries. These rulers are controlled by the Soviet government in Moscow. The Russians are quickly building up a new Soviet empire.

1945

May 1   **Hitler kills himself**
May 8   **Germany surrenders; VE Day**
August 7   **Atomic bomb dropped on Hiroshima**
August 15   **Japan surrenders**

Allies cross the Rhine

March 31, River Rhine, Germany American, British and Canadian troops have crossed the River Rhine in Germany. They are about to meet up with troops from the Russian army. The Allied and Russian armies will attack the Germans. The war in Europe is about to end.

Battles in Berlin

April 24, Berlin, Germany The Russian army has reached the German capital, Berlin. The Russians have surrounded the city. Hitler is hiding in an underground shelter somewhere in the city. Hitler still thinks that Germany can win the war. He is still giving orders to his armies. But he has only a million men to defend Berlin. Many are young boys, others are old men. The German airforce, the Luftwaffe, no longer exists.

△ The Russian flag flies in Berlin over the Reichstag, the parliament building.

Hitler is dead

May 1, Berlin, Germany Hitler is dead. He killed himself yesterday in his underground shelter in Berlin. The Italian leader, Mussolini, is also dead. He was shot three days ago.

Germany surrenders

May 8, Rheims, France The German leaders have surrendered to General Eisenhower in Rheims. The war in Europe is over. But the war with Japan continues.

△ A survivor from the Belsen concentration camp

London celebrates victory

May 8, London, England Today is Victory in Europe Day. It is called VE Day for short. The centre of London is full of people singing, dancing and cheering. The royal family stood on the balcony at Buckingham Palace this afternoon. They waved to the crowds of cheering people below. In Whitehall Prime Minister Churchill came out to see the crowd. The people sang 'For He's a Jolly Good Fellow' to him.

△ Celebrations in London on VE day

Inside the Belsen concentration camp

April 15, Belsen, Germany When the first Allied soldiers went into the concentration camps in Germany they were horrified by what they saw. Many thousands of Jewish people died in the concentration camps. This is how one soldier described what he saw:

"About 35,000 corpses were reckoned, more actually than the living. Of the living, there were about 30,000 . . .

The camp was so full because people had been brought here from east and west. Some people were brought from Nordhausen, a five-day journey, without food. Many had marched for two or three days. There was no food at all in the camp, a few piles of roots (vegetables) – amidst the piles of dead bodies. Some of the dead bodies were of people so hungry that though the roots were guarded by SS-men they had tried to storm them and had been shot down. There was no water. . ."

(Derek Sington, political officer, reported by Patrick Gordon-Walker in *Book of Reportage*, Faber 1987)

The forgotten war

May 19, Thailand British and Indian troops have driven the Japanese out of India and Burma. They are now about to invade Thailand. The British and Indian forces are led by General 'Bill' Slim. But in Europe many people have forgotten about the war in these countries. The papers have only written about the struggles in Europe and the Pacific.

Hiroshima destroyed

August 7, Washington, USA The Americans have dropped a new kind of bomb on the city of Hiroshima in Japan. An American B29 Superfortress plane dropped the bomb yesterday. It exploded with a huge, purple ball of fire. A dark cloud, shaped like a mushroom, rose from the bomb. This was an atomic bomb. It destroyed the city of Hiroshima. The bomb killed and injured thousands of people. The American President, Harry S. Truman, has threatened Japan with more atomic bombs unless it surrenders.

Japan surrenders

August 15, Tokyo, Japan On August 9, the Americans dropped another atomic bomb. It fell on Nagasaki in Japan and killed thousands of people. The Emperor of Japan has surrendered. This means that World War II is finally over.

△ Hiroshima after the bomb

Death in Hiroshima

September 9, Hiroshima, Japan This is a description of what happened when the atomic bomb dropped on Hiroshima: "Within a few seconds the thousands of people in the streets and the gardens in the centre of the town were scorched by a wave of searing heat. Many were killed instantly, others lay writhing on the ground screaming in agony from the intolerable pain of their burns. Trams were picked up and tossed aside as though they had neither weight nor solidity. Trains were flung off the rails as though they were toys. Horses, dogs and cattle suffered the same fate as human beings. Even the vegetation did not escape."

(Marcel Junod, *Warrior without Weapons*, Jonathan Cape 1951)

News in brief . . .

President dies suddenly

April 12, Washington, USA
President Roosevelt died suddenly today. The Vice-President Harry S. Truman will become the new president of the United States.

Lights shine in Britain

July 15, London, England
The blackout in Britain is over. During the blackout no lights were allowed at night in the streets, in shops or in buildings. The blackout made it more difficult for German planes to see where towns and cities were. Now streets and shops are lit up again.

▷ Clement Attlee, the leader of the Labour party

Countries work for peace

October 24, New York, USA
Twenty-nine countries have signed the United Nations Charter. This is an agreement to try to prevent war in the future.

▷ The symbol of the new United Nations.

Labour party win election

July 26, London, England
The Labour party has won the British election. The leader of the Labour party is Clement Attlee.

Germany and Berlin split up

August 2, Potsdam, Germany
The Allies are splitting Germany up. Different countries will control different areas of Germany. Leaders of the Allied countries are meeting at Potsdam. They have decided that Russia will take over the eastern half of Germany. The Americans, the British and the French will run the rest of the country. The German capital, Berlin, will be divided into four parts.

1946

The United Nations

January 10, London, England Today the United Nations is holding its first meeting. The Foreign Minister from Belgium, Paul Henri Spaak, will be the President of the United Nations. He was elected by one vote. The United States and the countries in the West voted for him. The USSR and the countries of the East wanted a different President. The countries of the West and East do not trust each other. This is very different to when they were Allies in the war.

Nazi leaders put on trial

September 30, Nuremberg, Germany The wartime Allies have put the Nazi leaders on trial. The trial is being held in Nuremberg, Germany. Eleven Nazi leaders have been sentenced to death. Eight will be put in prison.

Goering escapes hanging

October 16, Nuremberg, Germany Ten Nazi leaders were hanged this morning. But one of the leaders, Hermann Goering, escaped hanging. He killed himself by eating a poisonous pill.

△ Nazi leaders on trial at Nuremberg

Iron Curtain falls

March 5, Fulton, USA The countries of the East and the West are separating into two groups. These groups are often called 'blocs'. The Eastern bloc is controlled by the Communist government in the USSR. Eastern bloc countries include the USSR, Hungary Bulgaria, Romania, Poland, Czechoslovakia, Yugoslavia and the eastern part of Germany (see map). The East and West do not trust each other. Sir Winston Churchill has described the division between the two blocs as an 'Iron Curtain'.

> "A shadow has fallen upon the scenes so lately lighted by the Allied victory . . . From Stettin on the Baltic to Trieste on the Adriatic, an iron curtain has descended across Europe."

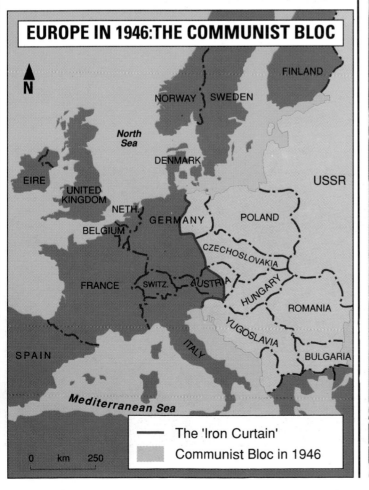

EUROPE IN 1946: THE COMMUNIST BLOC

N

FINLAND
NORWAY SWEDEN
North Sea
DENMARK
EIRE
UNITED KINGDOM
NETH.
GERMANY
BELGIUM
POLAND
USSR
CZECHOSLOVAKIA
FRANCE SWITZ. AUSTRIA
HUNGARY
ROMANIA
SPAIN
ITALY
YUGOSLAVIA
BULGARIA
Mediterranean Sea

—— The 'Iron Curtain'
▨ Communist Bloc in 1946
0   km   250

The United Nations bans the bomb

December 14, New York, USA All the members of the United Nations have voted to ban the atomic bomb. The United Nations want to prevent another atomic explosion like the ones at Hiroshima and Nagasaki.

▽ An atomic explosion

PEOPLE OF THE 30s AND 40s

Neville Chamberlain 1869–1940
Neville Chamberlain was the British Prime Minister when Britain entered the war in 1939. Chamberlain tried to persuade Hitler not to go to war. But Hitler fooled Chamberlain with his promises about Czechoslovakia (see page 18). In 1940, Chamberlain resigned and Winston Churchill took his place as Prime Minister. Chamberlain died of cancer in 1940.

Franklin D. Roosevelt 1882–1945
Franklin D. Roosevelt was President of the United States from 1933 to 1945. He led the United States into World War II in 1941. In 1944 he was elected President for the fourth time. He died in 1945, just before the war ended.

Walt Disney 1901–1966
Walt Disney was an American filmmaker. Many of his films were cartoons. He invented Mickey Mouse, Minnie Mouse, Donald Duck, Goofy, Pluto and many other characters.

Francisco Franco 1892–1975
Francisco Franco was the leader of Spain from 1937 until 1975. He organised the attack on the government which started the Spanish Civil War.

Adolf Hitler 1889–1945
Adolf Hitler was born in Austria, but he moved to Germany. He became leader of Germany in 1933. He ordered the invasions of Czechoslovakia, Austria and Poland. World War II followed. He killed himself in 1945, as the Russians entered Berlin.

Benito Mussolini 1883–1945
Benito Mussolini was the leader of Italy. Before this Mussolini was a teacher, then a journalist. He was on Hitler's side in World War II. But the Allies beat him in 1943. Mussolini was shot and killed in 1945.

Joseph Stalin 1879–1953
Joseph Stalin was the leader of the revolution in Russia in 1917. Millions of people died on his orders. In World War II, Stalin led Russia to victory over the Germans.

Winston Churchill 1874–1965

As a young man Winston Churchill was a soldier. He became a member of parliament in 1900. He was in the government during World War I. Churchill became unpopular after the war. This was because he kept giving warnings about the dangers of Communism and of Nazi Germany. He became the British Prime Minister in 1940. He led the British to victory in World War II. He wrote many books and won the Nobel Prize for Literature in 1953.

Charles de Gaulle 1890–1970

Charles de Gaulle escaped to England when the Germans captured France in 1940. From London he organised the French Resistance against the Germans. After the war he became the French President.

Viscount Montgomery 1887–1976

Viscount Montgomery's nickname was 'Monty'. He fought in World War I. In World War II he commanded troops in France and in Africa. He planned the battle of El Alamein against the German army. This battle ended with a victory for the Allies. It was an important turning point in the war. After this the Allies were able to advance on the Germans in North Africa.

Glossary

abdicate: to give up something formally, for example a throne.

Abyssinia: a country in northeast Africa now called Ethiopia.

air raid: an attack by enemy planes. The planes often dropped bombs.

the Allies: the countries that fought against Germany and Japan in World War II. The main Allied countries were Britain and the Commonwealth countries, the USA, Russia, France, China and Poland.

atomic bomb: a powerful bomb that causes much death and destruction.

Communists: Communists believe that all property and industry in a country should belong to the state.

concentration camps: camps built by the Nazis. The Nazis put their enemies in these camps. Millions of people died in concentration camps.

ghetto: in World War II an area of a city in which Jewish people were forced to live.

Luftwaffe: the German airforce. 'Luftwaffe' means 'air weapon'.

Nazi: the short name in German for 'The National Socialist German Worker's Party'.

Reichstag: the German parliament and the building it met in.

Resistance: in France the secret organisation that fought the Germans while the country was occupied.

treaty: an agreement between two or more countries.

Index